A Global Search and Find Book

CITIES AROUND THE WORLD

Illustrated by Tilly
Written by Lucy Menzies

IVY KIDS

CONTENTS

Barcelona 16

Rome 18

Moscow 20

Beijing 22

Tokyo 24

Sydney 26

Toronto 28

Answers 30

ABOUT THIS BOOK

You're about to visit some of the world's most exciting places. In this book, there are 12 incredible cities to explore. Each one has features that make it unique: architecture to examine, statues to admire, bridges to cross, streets to wander, food to taste and new people to meet.

First, learn about some of the most famous landmarks in the city, and find them in the scene. Search carefully, as they may be hidden behind other buildings. Then, look for the five extra things to spot in the picture. But watch out – in each city, one of the extra things to spot has decoys to trip you up! Once you've learned about the city, can you answer the special counting question on the page? When you've found everything, turn to the back of the book to check your answers, and discover even more information about the city.

Watch out for decoys - make sure you spot the exact one!

Look out for the special counting question in each city!

How many different squirrels can you find?

You don't need a passport or a plane ticket to go sightseeing; just flip to the first scene and start exploring.

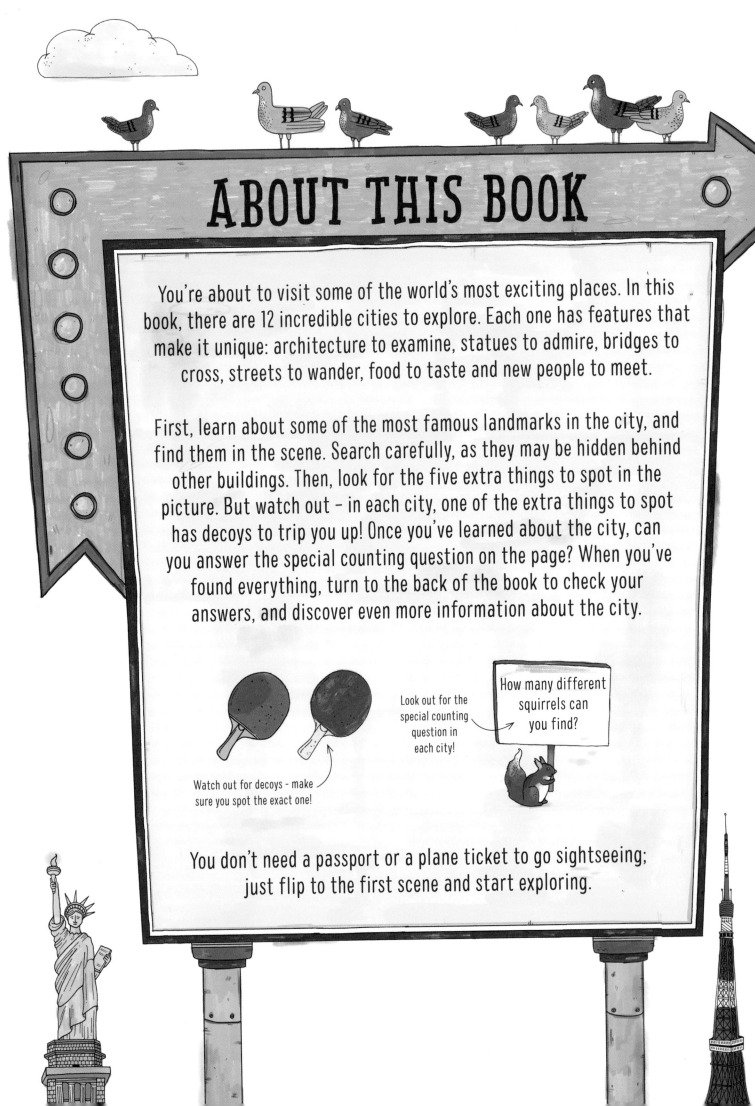

WHERE IN THE WORLD?

These 12 people each feature in a different city... but where in the world are they?
Can you spot them? Check your answers at the bottom of the page.

How many different pigeons can you find?

NEW YORK

Welcome to New York, the city that never sleeps. It has this nickname because it's buzzing with visitors, day and night. Explore Central Park, an enormous park in the heart of the city. Row a boat in the lake there, or visit the zoo inside! Then see the dazzlingly bright lights of Times Square. Flag down a yellow taxicab or ride the subway to get around.

CAN YOU FIND THESE LANDMARKS IN THE CITY?

STATUE OF LIBERTY
Lady Liberty was a gift from France to the US to celebrate America's independence from Great Britain. Climb the 377 steps inside the statue. From her crown, you'll get a spectacular view of the city.

EMPIRE STATE BUILDING
At 443 metres tall and with 102 floors, the Empire State Building is the 6th tallest building in the US. Completed in 1931, it's one of the most famous buildings on the New York skyline.

FLATIRON BUILDING
Originally called the Fuller Building, the Flatiron was renamed because of its triangular shape – it looks like a clothes iron!

BROOKLYN BRIDGE
This bridge connects two of New York's boroughs, Manhattan and Brooklyn. Cars drive across the bridge, but you can walk across it, too.

RADIO CITY MUSIC HALL
It may be a music hall, but this venue hosts films and plays as well as concerts. All the greats have played here, including Lady Gaga and The Rolling Stones.

GUGGENHEIM MUSEUM
This art gallery, opened in 1959, was designed by American architect Frank Lloyd Wright. Inside, a walkway spirals from floor to ceiling. It houses some of the most famous works of art in the world.

NOW SPOT THESE SIGHTS ACROSS NEW YORK:

Watch out for decoys! Make sure you spot this exact taxicab.

HOT DOG
It's said that the first hot dog was served in New York in 1867. Will you take a bite?

FIRE HYDRANT
Is it hot out today? If so, you might get lucky and see a fire hydrant spray water to help people cool down.

YELLOW TAXICAB
Thousands of these yellow taxicabs zoom along the streets of New York. Flag one down and hop in.

BROADWAY STARS
Go see a show on Broadway, the most famous theatre circuit in the world.

US FLAG
The US flag is known as the 'Stars and Stripes'. That's because of its 50 white stars and 13 red and white stripes.

BASEBALL
New York's two baseball teams, the Mets and the Yankees, have a fierce rivalry. Which will you root for?

LONDON

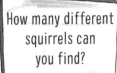

How many different squirrels can you find?

London is the capital city of the UK. It's packed full of fascinating history, stylish skyscrapers and famous residents. There's lots to see and do here! Travel the city on its speedy underground railway, known as the Tube, or sit on the top floor of a double-decker bus and get sightseeing. What can you find in London today?

CAN YOU FIND THESE LANDMARKS IN THE CITY?

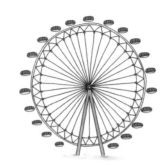

TOWER BRIDGE
Tower Bridge was built over 120 years ago. Its twin towers stand proudly in the River Thames. If you're there at the right time, you'll see an amazing sight – the bridge lifts in the middle to let ships sail down the river.

THE LONDON EYE
The London Eye is a huge Ferris wheel that stands on the south bank of the river. It can carry up to 800 people altogether. From the very top, you'll get a breathtaking view of the city.

BIG BEN
What time is it? Look up at London's most famous clock and you'll soon find out. Big Ben is the nickname of the enormous bell inside the clock tower, which is called Elizabeth Tower.

NELSON'S COLUMN
This is a monument to Admiral Horatio Nelson, who died in the Battle of Trafalgar in 1805. The column is 52 metres tall, and it features a statue of Nelson right at the top.

BUCKINGHAM PALACE
Queen Elizabeth II lives here. The palace has 775 rooms. This includes 78 bathrooms, 52 royal bedrooms, a doctor's surgery, a cinema, a post office and a pool!

THE GHERKIN
This skyscraper is a whopping 180 metres tall. Inside are shops, restaurants and offices. Can you guess why it's called The Gherkin? It's because it looks like a giant pickle!

NOW SPOT THESE SIGHTS ACROSS LONDON:

Watch out for decoys! Make sure you spot this exact post box.

PHONE BOX
Can you hear a phone ringing? Red phone boxes are dotted all across London.

TEACUP & SAUCER
Tea is a very popular drink in the UK. Try it in a traditional cup and saucer.

CORGI
Queen Elizabeth II has owned more than 30 corgis during her lifetime.

PEARLY KING & QUEEN
These two wear traditional outfits bejeweled with pearls to raise money for charity.

UK FLAG
The flag is also called the 'Union Jack'. It represents England and Wales, Scotland and Northern Ireland.

POST BOX
Mail your postcard in a red post box and it'll arrive safely back home.

AMSTERDAM

The capital of the Netherlands, Amsterdam, is full of canals. A great way to see the sights here is by river, so hop aboard a tour boat and wind your way through the city. What will you do today? Check out some fine art at the Van Gogh Museum, enjoy a tasty stroopwafel and marvel at the tall canal houses. Just look both ways on the street – there are bicycles everywhere!

CAN YOU FIND THESE LANDMARKS IN THE CITY?

RIJKSMUSEUM
This museum is dedicated to the history and art of Amsterdam. Inside, you can see many famous paintings and sculptures on display.

ANNE FRANK HOUSE
This is where Anne Frank and her family hid for two years during World War II. Millions of people visit here to learn about her life, and to commemorate her memory.

ROYAL PALACE
Before it became a royal residence in 1808, this amazing building was a town hall. Today, the royal family of the Netherlands uses the palace for important events.

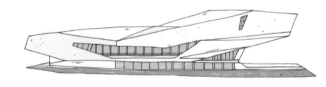

BLOEMENMARKT
Welcome to the world's one and only floating flower market. The market sits on the Singel canal and has been here since 1862. Look at all the flowers!

REMBRANDT STATUE IN REMBRANDTPLEIN
Rembrandt (1606–1669) was a Dutch artist who lived in the city. He is famous for the dramatic way he painted light and shadows in his portraits. This technique is known as chiaroscuro.

EYE FILMMUSEUM
This super-cool building is a film museum. Its collection is made up of films, posters, photographs and books. Opened in 2010, the building sits on the IJ Harbour.

NOW SPOT THESE SIGHTS ACROSS AMSTERDAM:

Watch out for decoys! Make sure you spot this exact chess piece.

A SOCIAL SOFA
You'll find these benches, shaped like sofas, across the city. Their purpose is to bring neighbours together.

TULIPS
These flowers are very popular in the Netherlands. Find them in the Bloemenmarkt.

A WINDMILL
There are hundreds of windmills across the Netherlands.

A KORFBALL HOOP
Korfball is a Dutch sport similar to basketball. It was invented in 1902 by Nico Broekhuysen.

DUTCH FLAG
The Dutch flag is made up of red, white and blue horizontal stripes.

CHESS PIECE
Chess is very popular in the Netherlands! At Amsterdam's chess museum, you can play a game on a huge board.

PARIS

Bonjour! You're in Paris, the capital of France. There are fine art galleries and museums, mouth-watering pâtisseries, fashionable people and pretty streets. The Eiffel Tower is one of the most famous landmarks here. Take the lift right to the top and feast your eyes on the city below.

CAN YOU FIND THESE LANDMARKS IN THE CITY?

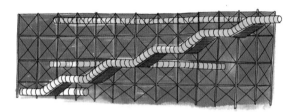

POMPIDOU CENTRE
The Pompidou Centre is a gallery filled with fascinating pieces of modern art. But it's interesting to look at on the outside, too, as colourful pipes snake across the building.

SACRÉ-COEUR
The white domes of the Sacré-Coeur sit atop a hill in the Montmartre district. It's a steep climb to reach this church, but you can hop on its funicular – a cable car that moves at an angle – and ride to the top to take in the spectacular view.

EIFFEL TOWER
When the tower was finished in 1889, some Parisians thought it was ugly! Now it's one of the most famous structures in the world and people flock here to see it.

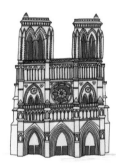

ARC DE TRIOMPHE
This towering archway was built in tribute to those who died fighting for France during various wars in the 1700s and 1800s. It was commissioned by Emperor Napoléon Bonaparte and took an amazing 30 years to build!

THE LOUVRE
This popular museum is home to one of the most famous paintings in the world, Leonardo da Vinci's *Mona Lisa*. Outside, there is a huge glass pyramid.

NOTRE-DAME
Notre-Dame cathedral is covered in stone gargoyles that are pulling funny faces. It has beautiful stained-glass windows and huge bells. In 2019, the cathedral was damaged by fire but work is underway to rebuild the parts that were burned.

NOW SPOT THESE SIGHTS ACROSS PARIS:

Watch out for decoys! Make sure you spot this exact brush.

CROISSANT
This crescent-shaped breakfast food is made with pastry and lots of butter, and is served for breakfast.

ARTIST'S PAINTBRUSH
Many famous artists have lived in Paris, including Pablo Picasso and Claude Monet.

FASHIONISTA
Paris is one of the fashion capitals of the world. Can you spot this stylish lady?

METRO SIGN
Is this a flower about to bloom? No – it's an entrance to the city's underground railway!

FRENCH FLAG
The blue, white and red of France's national flag can be seen all across the city. The French call it the Tricolore.

TOUR DE FRANCE CYCLIST
This cycling race, held across France every year, finishes in Paris.

How many iced gingerbread cookies can you count?

BERLIN

Brrrr! It's snowy and cold in Berlin today. We're at the Fernsehturm, an iconic tower that can be seen from miles around. There's lots to see and do in the city. Will you take a boat cruise on the River Spree? Or take a stroll around the Gendarmenmarkt, a beautiful public square? Just be sure to grab your hat and scarf before you begin to explore.

CAN YOU FIND THESE LANDMARKS IN THE CITY?

TEMPODROM
This music venue, at Potsdamer Platz, looks like a huge tent! It hosts all kinds of different events, from rock concerts to sports championships.

CHARLOTTENBURG PALACE
This incredible palace, completed in 1713, is named after Queen Sophia Charlotte. Royalty used to live here, but today it is open to visitors.

THE FERNSEHTURM
This tower stands tall over the city. From here, television is broadcast to the people of Germany. The silver sphere is actually an observation deck that rotates 360°.

BODE MUSEUM
The Bode Museum sits on Museum Island, a small island on the River Spree. The museum, opened in 1904, is famous for its amazing collection of coins.

REICHSTAG
The government of Germany meets here. The Reichstag took ten years to build and was finished in 1894. You can visit its amazing glass dome and look out across Berlin.

BRANDENBURG GATE
The Brandenburg Gate is an iconic German structure, and lots of important events throughout history have happened here. It was built between 1788 and 1791.

NOW SPOT THESE SIGHTS ACROSS BERLIN:

Watch out for decoys! Make sure you spot this exact table tennis bat.

U-BAHN TRAIN
The U-Bahn trains, which run both underground and overground, will take you all across the city.

TABLE TENNIS BAT
Table tennis is a popular pastime in Berlin – watch out for people playing it in city parks.

A PRETZEL
Dough is wrapped into a knot shape and then baked to produce this tasty German bread.

CURRYWURST
This snack was first made in Berlin. It is chopped sausage (or wurst) and curry sauce.

GERMAN FLAG
The flag of Germany features the country's three national colours: black, red and gold.

BEAR
The bear is the symbol of the city. You can see a bear on Berlin's coat of arms.

How many different fans can you see?

BARCELONA

When you visit Barcelona in Spain, you'll taste mouth-watering food, watch flamenco dancers perform and see some of the most astounding architecture in the world. But perhaps best of all, this is a city with a beach! Take a dip in the warm Mediterranean Sea, make a sandcastle, or have a siesta (that's a nap) in the shade. There's plenty to do in this Spanish city.

CAN YOU FIND THESE LANDMARKS IN THE CITY?

MAGIC FOUNTAIN OF MONTJUÏC
Can you see the fountain's powerful jets of water shoot up into the air? One jet reaches 50 metres high! At night, there are amazing water displays with lights and music.

SAGRADA FAMILIA
Construction began on this amazing church in 1882... and it's still ongoing! It's expected to be completed in 2026. It was designed by Spanish architect Antoni Gaudí, one of the most celebrated architects in history. His work can be spotted all around the city, but this church is seen as his masterpiece.

TORRE GLÒRIES
Torre Glòries is a 38-storey skyscraper. There are almost 4,500 LED lights on the outside of the building, which can be programmed to create many different colours and patterns.

PLAÇA D'ESPAÑA
This square is one of the busiest in Spain and at 34,000 square metres, it is one of the largest. Right at the centre is a fountain, designed by Spanish architect Josep Maria Jujol.

THE FAT CAT
This huge cat sculpture was made by Colombian artist Fernando Botero. It lives in Barcelona's Raval neighbourhood. Do you like its huge features?

CASA BATLLÓ
Another of Gaudí's wonders, this building is a piece of art. It is covered with a mosaic made of broken ceramic tiles. The inside space is used to host cultural events.

NOW SPOT THESE SIGHTS ACROSS BARCELONA:

Watch out for decoys! Make sure you spot this exact football.

CABLE CARS
Ride one of these cable cars high into the sky and get an amazing view of the city.

CHURROS
This tasty treat is made from deep-fried pastry dough.

PARK GÜELL
These buildings stand in Park Güell. They are yet another example of Gaudí's work in Barcelona.

A FOOTBALL
FC Barcelona is one of the best football teams in the world. Watch them play at their ground, Camp Nou.

A 'LIVING STATUE'
These performers on the La Rambla street stay perfectly still, like statues. Wait – did you see him move?

TOWER OF PEOPLE
In this traditional event, people climb on top of each other to make a tall tower, known as a 'castell'.

ROME

How many different cameras can you find (including phone cameras)?

You can see Rome's history just about everywhere you turn. It's a city full of beautiful fountains, churches and statues. It was founded by the ancient Romans and was the capital of the Roman Empire. Many of their incredible buildings, such as the Colosseum, are still standing. Grab yourself some gelato (ice cream) and gaze up at this wonder of the world.

CAN YOU FIND THESE LANDMARKS IN THE CITY?

THE COLOSSEUM
This amazing arena is almost 2,000 years old and was built during the ancient Roman era. Lots of people came here to watch fights between Roman warriors, called gladiators.

THE TREVI FOUNTAIN
People gather around this beautiful fountain to cool down during the summer heat. Legend says that if you throw a coin into the fountain, you are sure to return to Rome one day!

THE COLUMN OF MARCUS AURELIUS
This tall column was built in tribute to a great Roman emperor, Marcus Aurelius. Pictures carved around the column tell the story of his victories in battle.

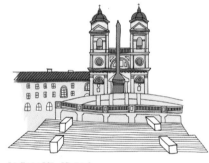

ROMAN FORUM
The Forum was at the centre of daily life in ancient Rome. There were market stalls, temples and public meetings here. But all that's left of it today are ruins.

ST PETER'S BASILICA
This is one of the biggest churches in the world. It's part of the Vatican, which is the headquarters of the Catholic church. Millions of people come here to pray every year.

SPANISH STEPS
Tourists sit on these steps and enjoy the city. But there's a strict rule – you may not eat or drink while sitting here! This is to keep them clean and tidy.

NOW SPOT THESE SIGHTS ACROSS ROME:

Watch out for decoys! Make sure you spot this exact helmet.

SPAGHETTI
There are hundreds of different kinds of pasta in Italy, but spaghetti is Rome's speciality.

A SCOOTER HELMET
You'll see people zipping around on scooters all across the city.

ROMAN SHE-WOLF
Legend has it that the two founders of the city, Romulus and Remus, were raised by a wolf.

NASONI DRINKING FOUNTAIN
There are nearly 3,000 of these drinking fountains dotted all across Rome.

ITALIAN FLAG
Some people say the green of the flag represents hope; the white, faith; and the red, charity.

CAT
It's a long-held tradition here that cats have the freedom of the city, and can roam wherever they please.

How many people are wearing hats?

MOSCOW

We're in Moscow's Red Square, the heart of this city. The square is surrounded by very important buildings, including The Kremlin and St Basil's Cathedral. Moscow is Russia's capital city, and it's huge – nearly 17 million people live here! It's one of the biggest cities in the world, meaning that there's a lot to see and do. So – what are you waiting for?

CAN YOU FIND THESE LANDMARKS IN THE CITY?

THE KREMLIN
This is where Russia's president lives. The Kremlin is made up of lots of different buildings, including Spasskaya Tower, a gateway into the Kremlin complex.

EVOLUTION TOWER
Evolution Tower is 55 storeys tall. It looks like it is twisting! It was designed by British architect, Tony Kettle. Inside the building there are offices and shops.

ST BASIL'S CATHEDRAL
Can you see the amazing striped domes of St Basil's? They were designed to look like flames rising into the sky. St Basil's used to be a place of worship, but now it's a museum.

BOLSHOI THEATRE
Some of the world's finest performances are held here. Built between 1821 and 1824, the theatre has its own ballet and opera companies, and its own orchestra.

MONUMENT TO YURI GAGARIN
Russian astronaut Yuri Gagarin was the first person to travel into space. His spacecraft orbited Earth in 1961. This monument, made from titanium, has a statue of him at the top.

GUM STORE
This beautiful building has been a department store for more than a hundred years. It is topped with a stunning glass roof. Inside, there are lots of shops to buy souvenirs from.

NOW SPOT THESE SIGHTS ACROSS MOSCOW:

Watch out for decoys! Make sure you spot this exact balalaika.

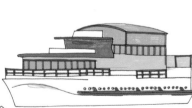

ICE SKATER
During the winter months, you can skate across an enormous ice rink in the Red Square. Yippee!

BALALAIKA
This triangular-shaped instrument is similar to the guitar. It is used to play traditional Russian folk music.

BALLET SHOES
Moscow is famous for its graceful ballerinas. Can you find this pair of ballet shoes?

CIRCUS PERFORMER
Moscow is world-famous for its circus, where acrobats such as this one perform amazing tricks.

RUSSIAN FLAG
The white, blue and red stripes have been part of Russia's official flag design since 1993.

SIGHTSEEING BOAT
Take a trip on a boat down the River Moskva, which snakes its way through the city centre.

How many different lanterns can you count?

BEIJING

We're in Beijing, the capital city of China. Tonight, the people here are enjoying Spring Festival, a holiday celebrated every year. There's food, music and a huge parade with dragon dancing, a traditional Chinese dance. Look – there are even fireworks! Can you hear them whizz and bang?

CAN YOU FIND THESE LANDMARKS IN THE CITY?

BIRD'S NEST (BEIJING NATIONAL STADIUM)
The Beijing National Stadium was built for the 2008 Beijing Olympics. The criss-cross design of the building makes it look like a bird's nest.

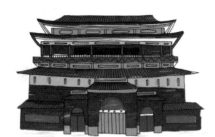

THE DRUM TOWER
This wooden tower was built in 1272. It housed a set of 24 drums that were initially used for music, and later as way of telling the time. Only one of the original drums survives today.

DESHENGMEN
The city of Beijing was surrounded by a wall until 1953. Deshengmen, a former gate tower, is one of the few parts of the wall that still survives today.

FORBIDDEN CITY
For 500 years, until 1912, this was a palace that housed the Emperor of China. It's now a museum, so you can visit and see its beautiful rooms and lush gardens for yourself.

CCTV BUILDING
This is a very strange-shaped skyscraper. Built in 2008, it's an office building in the centre of Beijing's business district. From certain angles, it looks like a pair of trousers!

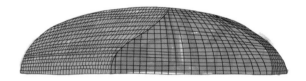

NATIONAL CENTRE FOR THE PERFORMING ARTS
This building is a theatre that can seat over 5,000 people. It's known as 'The Giant Egg' because of its shape. The theatre is surrounded by an artificial lake.

NOW SPOT THESE SIGHTS ACROSS BEIJING:

Watch out for decoys! Make sure you spot this exact panda.

XUN
This egg-shaped flute is an instrument that has been played in China for thousands of years.

GIANT PANDA
The giant panda is a famous Chinese symbol. Beijing Zoo houses some of these amazing creatures.

A RED ENVELOPE
During Spring Festival, it is tradition to give gifts of money in a red envelope.

A DUMPLING
A traditional food, dumplings are steamed parcels of dough filled with vegetables or meat.

CHINESE FLAG
China's national flag is red and features five golden stars.

KUNG FU
Kung fu, or martial arts, began in China. It is practised for self-defence and exercise.

How many different origami birds can you spot?

TOKYO

Tokyo is big, busy and bright. There are enormous skyscrapers and lots of futuristic-looking buildings. You can also find ancient temples, and the delicate pink flowers of the cherry trees that blossom in springtime. Here we are at the famous Shibuya road crossing, and it's rush hour. Look at all of the hustle and bustle!

CAN YOU FIND THESE LANDMARKS IN THE CITY?

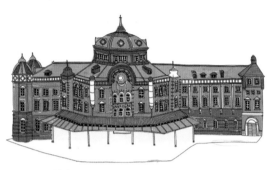

TOKYO STATION
This is the city's main railway terminal. Here, you can catch a super-fast bullet train, which is able to travel at speeds of up to 320 kilometres per hour!

MODE GAKUEN COCOON TOWER
The lattice pattern around this skyscraper makes it look like a cocoon! This amazing building is actually a school, and people come here to study all kinds of subjects.

TOKYO TOWER
This tower is painted orange and white so that it's visible to aeroplanes. The tower is an antenna that transmits television and radio signals all across the city.

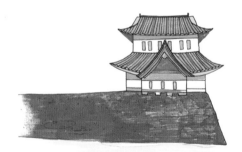

IMPERIAL PALACE
The Emperor of Japan lives in this palace. It's surrounded by a moat (a wide ditch filled with water). You can take a tour around the lush gardens of the palace.

TOKYO SKYTREE
At 634 metres, this is one of the tallest towers in the world. It broadcasts radio and television signals. Inside, there is a glass floor that lets you look down at the city below. Woah!

NAKAGIN CAPSULE TOWER
Inside this building are capsules, tiny cube-shaped rooms, designed for people to live in. Today, most of the capsules are uninhabited and some have been abandoned and left to ruin, but it's still a notable work of architecture.

NOW SPOT THESE SIGHTS ACROSS TOKYO:

Watch out for decoys! Make sure you spot this exact lucky cat.

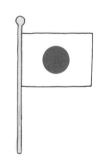

SUSHI
This Japanese delicacy is made with rice, seaweed and raw fish.

LUCKY CAT (MANEKI-NEKO)
Cat figurines are very popular here and are kept as good luck charms.

GETA SHOE
These sandals are like flip-flops made of wood. They have blocks attached to the underside.

HARAJUKU FASHIONISTA
This eccentric style of fashion can be seen on the streets of the Harajuku district.

JAPANESE FLAG
Japan's national flag features a red circle. This symbolizes the rising sun.

HACHIKŌ STATUE
This is a tribute to Hachikō, a loyal dog who waited in the same spot every day for nine years for his owner after they passed away.

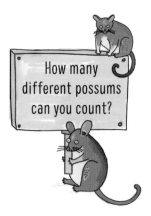

How many different possums can you count?

SYDNEY

Grab your hat and sunglasses – we're in Sydney and the sun is shining! At the city's world-famous harbour, there are boats in the water and lots of people are enjoying the summer. Take a stroll along the waterfront and see the opera house up-close. Or perhaps you could get in the water yourself and do some kayaking! Just be sure to keep cool in Australia's scorching heat.

CAN YOU FIND THESE LANDMARKS IN THE CITY?

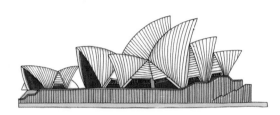

SYDNEY OPERA HOUSE
The Sydney Opera House opened in 1973 and took 14 years to build. Inside, there are nearly 1,000 rooms in which all kinds of performances, from ballet to circus acts, are held.

SYDNEY HARBOUR BRIDGE
This bridge connects the north and south of the city. Opened in 1932, it took eight years to build. At 134 metres, it is the largest steel arch bridge in the world.

SYDNEY TOWER
At 309 metres, this golden tower is the tallest building on the Sydney skyline. At the very top is an observation deck, from which you can see all of the city below.

CULWULLA CHAMBERS
Completed in 1912, Culwulla Chambers is Australia's first and oldest skyscraper. But compared to other buildings around the world, it is relatively small at 50 metres high.

THE BIG MATCHSTICKS
This 8-metre high sculpture, created by Australian artist Brett Whiteley, is actually called *Almost Once*, but people call it 'The Big Matchsticks' because that's what it looks like – one burnt and one unburnt. It is made from wood and fibreglass.

ANZAC MEMORIAL
This memorial, in Sydney's Hyde Park, stands in tribute to soldiers from Australia and New Zealand who fought and died in World War I.

NOW SPOT THESE SIGHTS ACROSS SYDNEY:

COCKATOO
This white-breasted bird with a yellow crest calls Sydney its home.

EL ALAMEIN MEMORIAL FOUNTAIN
This incredible bronze fountain resembles a dandelion flower spreading its seeds.

BIRDCAGES
Visit Angel Place and you'll see *Forgotten Songs*, an art installation made with over 100 birdcages.

Watch out for decoys! Make sure you spot this exact cricket ball.

CRICKET BALL
Australia loves cricket! You can see a game at the Sydney Cricket Ground.

AUSTRALIAN FLAG
The flag features the Union Jack, as well as stars that represent the Southern Cross constellation.

A BOOMERANG
When you throw this curved stick, it will come back to you! It was used for hunting by indigenous Australians.

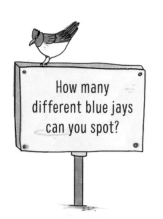

How many different blue jays can you spot?

TORONTO

It's a beautiful autumnal day in Toronto, and we're on the waterside of Lake Ontario. This Canadian city has the most diverse population in the world. What will you do here? You could watch an ice-hockey game, or visit the Bata Shoe Museum – that's right, a museum filled with shoes! Toronto is full of amazing sights, so get your (hockey) skates on and get exploring.

CAN YOU FIND THESE LANDMARKS IN THE CITY?

PRINCES' GATE
This amazing stone gateway was built to commemorate the 60th anniversary of Canada becoming a country. Atop the central arch stands the Goddess of Winged Victory statue.

GOODERHAM BUILDING
The Gooderham Building was completed in 1892. Its triangular shape is an example of 'flatiron' architecture of the early 20th century. It is just 17 metres tall!

CN TOWER
This impressive tower is a focal point of the Toronto skyline. It's one of the tallest free-standing structures in the world. Climb its 1,776 steps to the top for an amazing view.

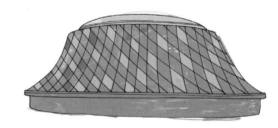

ROYAL ONTARIO MUSEUM
One of the most-visited museums in Canada, this incredible crystal shaped museum houses important historical and scientific exhibits.

HOCKEY HALL OF FAME
If you're an ice-hockey fan, you'll love the Hockey Hall of Fame. It's a museum dedicated to the history of the sport and is filled with all kinds of fascinating memorabilia.

ROY THOMSON HALL
The Roy Thomson Hall seats over 2,500 people. Opened in 1982, music of all different kinds is performed here. Inside is an enormous pipe organ specially built for the venue.

NOW SPOT THESE SIGHTS ACROSS TORONTO:

Watch out for decoys! Make sure you spot this exact cannon.

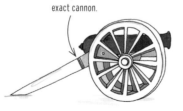

TRAM
Trams have been carrying people around the city since 1861.

A HOCKEY PUCK
Toronto has its own ice hockey team, the Maple Leafs. Catch them at the Scotiabank Arena.

CANNON
At Fort York, a historical military base, you'll see cannons that were once used in battle.

BEAVER
The beaver features on the city's coat of arms to represent the spirit of its hardworking citizens.

CANADIAN FLAG
The flag of Canada features a maple leaf, a tree native to the country.

MINI DOUGHNUTS
These yummy, tiny doughnuts are a Toronto tradition.

ANSWERS

NEW YORK

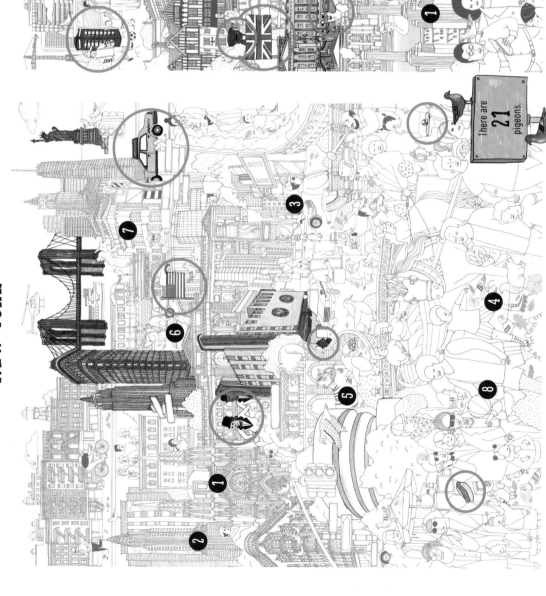

There are **21** pigeons.

LONDON

There are **3** squirrels.

EXTRA THINGS TO DISCOVER IN NEW YORK:

1 **ST PATRICK'S CATHEDRAL** A Roman Catholic Gothic-style church

2 **CHRYSLER BUILDING** A 77-storey tall skyscraper

3 **TIMES SQUARE** A popular public square filled with shops, restaurants and billboards

4 **CENTRAL PARK** A park with many attractions, including gardens, lakes, statues and performance spaces

5 **CENTRAL PARK ZOO** A small zoo within Central Park, first opened in 1864

6 **GEORGE WASHINGTON STATUE** A statue of America's first president in Union Square

7 **CHINATOWN** A neighbourhood that is home to Chinese food and culture

8 **BASKETBALL** NYC has two basketball teams: the Knicks and the Nets

EXTRA THINGS TO DISCOVER IN LONDON:

1 **BATTERSEA POWER STATION** Formerly an electricity station, now converted into homes, offices, restaurants and shops

2 **SHARD** A 95-storey tall skyscraper

3 **SHAKESPEARE'S GLOBE** A reconstruction of English writer William Shakespeare's theatre, where visitors can watch performances of his plays

4 **ST PAUL'S CATHEDRAL** One of the most famous landmarks in the city. Visitors can climb 528 steps all the way to the top of the church's dome

5 **LIBERTY** A huge department store with a mock Tudor-style exterior

6 **TOWER OF LONDON** This castle was used as a prison for over 850 years. Today, it houses the crown jewels

7 **ELEPHANT AND CASTLE** This statue stands at the Elephant and Castle tube station in south London

8 **20 FENCHURCH STREET** A skyscraper nicknamed the 'Walkie-Talkie' because of its shape

9 **IMPERIAL WAR MUSEUM** A museum filled with artefacts from World War I onwards

AMSTERDAM

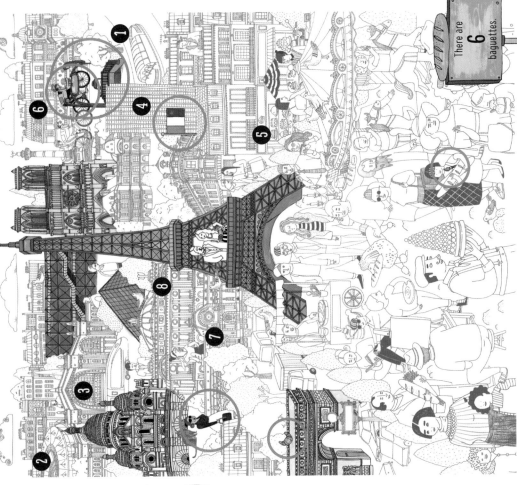

EXTRA THINGS TO DISCOVER IN AMSTERDAM:

1. **CLOG** A traditional Dutch wooden shoe

2. **TRAM** Trams are a popular mode of transport here and can be found all across the city

3. **CITY ARCHIVES** This huge building houses collections of important documents on shelving that extends for almost 50 kilometres

4. **ANNE FRANK STATUE** A statue of Anne Frank stands near the house where she wrote her diary

5. **HERMITAGE AMSTERDAM** A museum that is an extension of the Hermitage in St Petersburg, Russia, which exhibits collections of Russian and Dutch art

6. **NATIONAL MONUMENT** A memorial to the fallen soldiers of World War II

7. **CENTRAAL STATION** The city's main railway station

8. **WAAG** Now a restaurant, originally a 15th-century gate in the wall that surrounded the city

9. **HERON** Grey herons call Amsterdam home

There are 13 bicycles.

PARIS

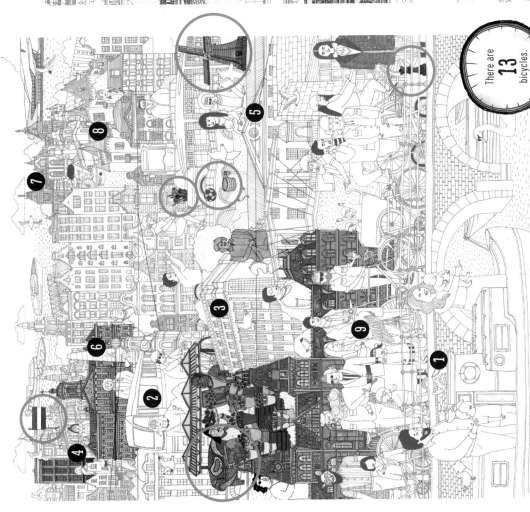

EXTRA THINGS TO DISCOVER IN PARIS:

1. **RIVER SEINE** The second longest river in France. It flows through the city and people stroll along its banks and take boat trips

2. **STADE DE FRANCE** France's national sports stadium

3. **PARIS-NORD** A major railway station – the busiest in Europe

4. **TOUR MONTPARNASSE** A 59-storey tall skyscraper

5. **PÂTISSERIES** These French bakeries are found all around the city. They specialise in sweet treats

6. **PARIS-GARE-DE-LYON** Another major railway station named after another French city – Lyon

7. **MUSÉE D'ORSAY** A railway station turned museum that houses art, including major works by artists such as Monet

8. **PALAIS GARNIER** An opera house that can seat nearly 2,000 people

There are 6 baguettes.

BARCELONA

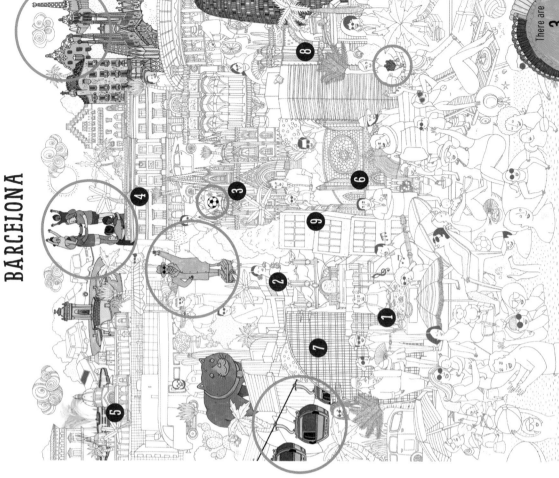

There are **3** fans.

EXTRA THINGS TO DISCOVER IN BARCELONA:

1. **PAELLA** A Spanish dish made from rice, vegetables, meat or seafood
2. **FLAMENCO DANCER** A dancer who performs flamenco, a traditional Spanish dance
3. **CATHEDRAL OF BARCELONA** A Catholic church with a range of gargoyles perched on its roof, including mythical beasts
4. **CITY HALL** Barcelona's city hall
5. **MUSEU NACIONAL D'ART DE CATALUNYA** A gallery that houses art from Catalonia (Barcelona is in the region of Catalonia)
6. **SANTA MARIA DEL MAR** A Catholic church completed in 1383
7. **W BARCELONA** A super-tall hotel on the water front
8. **ARCO DE TRIUNFO** A red brick arch built in 1888 decorated with sculptures of lions, bats and angels
9. **HOMENATGE A LA BARCELONETA** A beachfront sculpture built for the 1992 Olympics

BERLIN

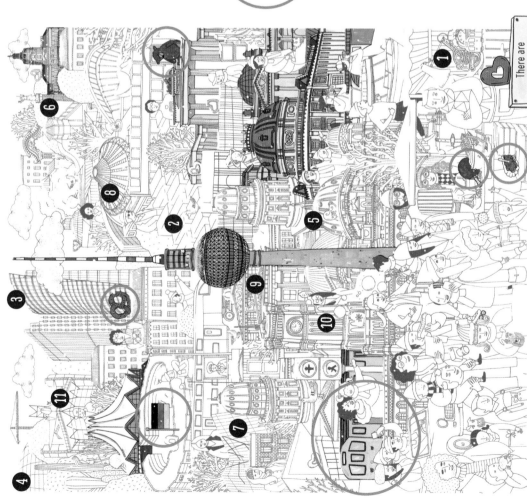

There are **13** gingerbread cookies.

EXTRA THINGS TO DISCOVER IN BERLIN:

1. **FLEA MARKET** A market of second-hand goods is held every Sunday at Mauerpark
2. **HOLOCAUST MEMORIAL** A memorial to Jewish people who died in World War II
3. **BAHN-TOWER** A 26-storey tall skyscraper
4. **BERLIN BRAIN** A library dedicated to philology (the study of languages)
5. **BERLIN CATHEDRAL CHURCH** A Protestant church and one of the key landmarks in Berlin's cityscape
6. **PEACE COLUMN** A 19-metre column topped with Victoria, Roman goddess of Victory
7. **JEWISH MUSEUM** A museum dedicated to Jewish culture
8. **SONY CENTRE** An entertainment complex in Potsdamer Platz
9. **GENDARMENMARKT** A public square with a domed church on either side
10. **ROTES RATHAUS** Berlin's town hall
11. **GERMAN MUSEUM OF TECHNOLOGY** A museum filled with scientific and technological artefacts

ROME

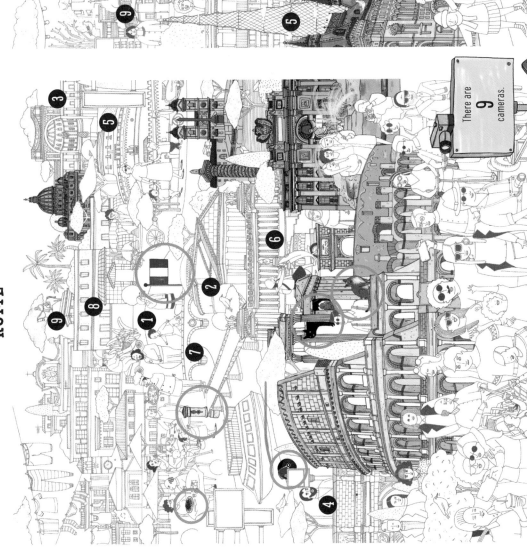

There are **9** cameras.

EXTRA THINGS TO DISCOVER IN ROME:

1. **RIVER TIBER** A river that flows through the city
2. **PANTHEON** Formerly a Roman temple, it is now a Catholic church with a circular hole at the centre of its dome – when it rains the water falls straight into the church
3. **VATICAN MUSEUMS** Two museums within the Vatican filled with art
4. **CATHOLICISM** Rome has been a centre for Catholicism for centuries and today thousands of worshippers, including nuns and priests, visit the city
5. **CASTEL SANT'ANGELO** Formerly a fortress, it is now a museum
6. **PIAZZA VENEZIA** A beautiful square featuring a monument to an Italian king, Victor Emmanuel II
7. **PONTE SISTO** A bridge that has spanned the River Tiber since the 15th century
8. **ORTO BOTANICO** A botanical garden in the city
9. **MONUMENT TO GARIBALDI** A statue dedicated to Giuseppe Garibaldi, an Italian general

MOSCOW

18 people are wearing hats.

EXTRA THINGS TO DISCOVER IN MOSCOW:

1. **EDELWEISS** A 43-storey residential skyscraper
2. **HOTEL UKRAINA** A luxury hotel with 497 rooms
3. **MOSCOW STATE UNIVERSITY** Moscow's university building
4. **PUSHKIN MUSEUM** A museum that houses fine art
5. **SHUKHOV TOWER** A 160-metre tall broadcasting tower
6. **MOSKOVSKY ZOOPARK** A large zoo in the centre of Moscow that was founded in 1864
7. **LUZHNIKI STADIUM** An 81,000-seater football stadium – the biggest in Russia
8. **TRIUMPHAL ARCH** An archway built to celebrate Russia's victory over the French after their invasion in 1812
9. **DONSKOY MONASTERY** This monastery is occupied by Russian Orthodox monks
10. **NOVODEVICHY CONVENT** This convent is occupied by Russian Orthodox nuns

BEIJING

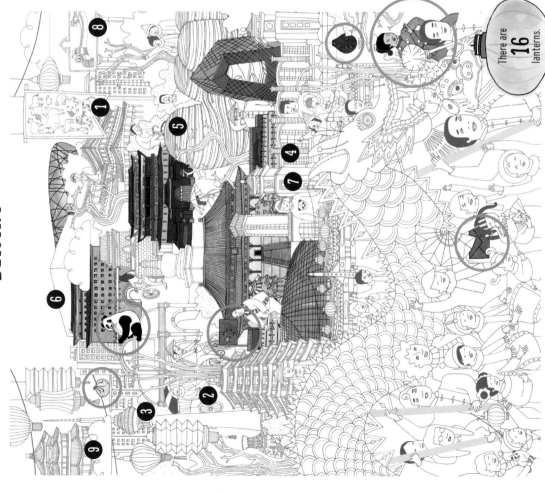

There are **16** lanterns.

EXTRA THINGS TO DISCOVER IN BEIJING:

1. **CHINESE ZODIAC CHART** The Chinese zodiac is based on a repeating 12-year cycle with a different animal assigned to each year

2. **RICKSHAW** This is a popular way to travel around the city. Passengers in carts are towed along by cyclists

3. **TV TOWER** A huge tower that transmits TV and radio signals

4. **BEIJING STATION** A major railway station within the city which features two giant clock towers

5. **GALAXY SOHO** A three-tower complex made up of homes, offices and shops

6. **BEIJING NATIONAL AQUATICS CENTRE** Nicknamed the 'Water Cube', this venue was built to host swimming events in the 2008 Olympics

7. **MONUMENT TO THE PEOPLE'S HEROES** A monument at Tiananmen Square dedicated to those who died during different wars in China

8. **GREAT WALL OF CHINA** This wonder of the world is located to the north of the city

9. **SUMMER PALACE** A large complex of palaces, gardens and lakes

TOKYO

There are **15** origami birds.

EXTRA THINGS TO DISCOVER IN TOKYO:

1. **METROPOLITAN GOVERNMENT BUILDING** The headquarters of Tokyo's local government

2. **MASCOTS** Characters created to advertise businesses and events

3. **CHERRY BLOSSOM** These pink flowers from Japanese cherry trees blossom all around the city during springtime

4. **HARAJUKU** A neighbourhood famous for its colourful fashion and street art

5. **ROBOT** Robots are very popular here and can be seen in restaurants, hotels and museums

6. **BULLET TRAIN** These superfast trains don't have wheels – they are raised above the tracks by magnets

7. **AKASAKA PALACE** A palace used to host important international visitors

8. **THE NATIONAL ART CENTRE** A gallery filled with temporary art exhibits

9. **SHINJUKU PARK TOWER** A huge single building made up of three blocks. Inside are shops, flats, offices and a hotel

TORONTO

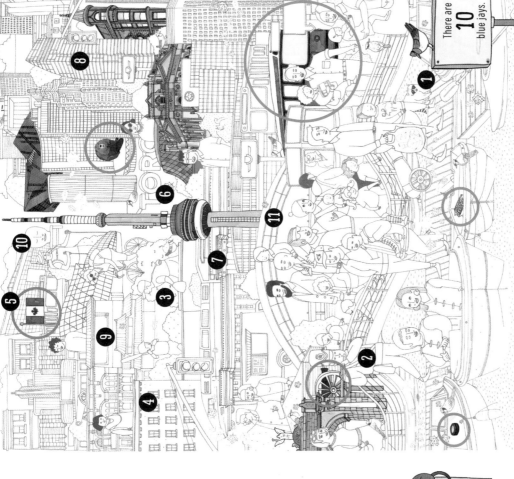

There are **10** blue jays.

EXTRA THINGS TO DISCOVER IN TORONTO:

1 **RACOON** A small wild mammal that has made the city its home

2 **FORT YORK** A historic military base where the roles of soldiers from the war of 1812 are re-enacted

3 **TORONTO BLUE JAYS** The city's baseball team

4 **GRAFFITI ALLEY** A street famous for its graffiti artwork

5 **BATA SHOE MUSEUM** A museum dedicated solely to footwear

6 **TORONTO SIGN** A 3D sign created for the 2015 Pan American Games

7 **UNION STATION** The city's main railway station

8 **L TOWER** A skyscraper containing 600 flats

9 **CHINATOWN** A neighbourhood home to Chinese food and culture

10 **GARDINER MUSEUM** Outside this museum of ceramics is a giant head made of glazed ceramic

11 **ROGERS CENTRE** An arena used to host sports such as baseball, basketball and football

SYDNEY

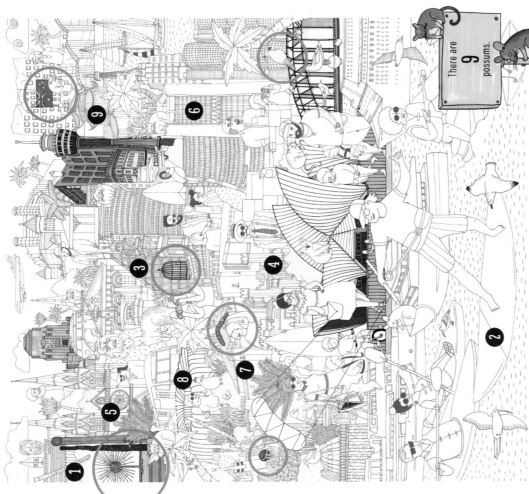

There are **9** possums.

EXTRA THINGS TO DISCOVER IN SYDNEY:

1 **DIDGERIDOO** A wind instrument crafted and played by indigenous Australian people

2 **WATER SPORTS** Sydney Harbour is often packed with kayakers, wind surfers and jet skiers

3 **DEUTSCHE BANK PLACE** A 39-storey skyscraper

4 **GOVERNMENT HOUSE** An official Australian government residence

5 **ST MARY'S CATHEDRAL** A Roman Catholic church

6 **SUNCORP PLACE** A 48-storey skyscraper

7 **SYDNEY CONSERVATORIUM** A school of music

8 **THE CALYX** An event space within The Royal Botanic Garden

9 **CHINESE GARDEN OF FRIENDSHIP** A park modelled on traditional Chinese gardens

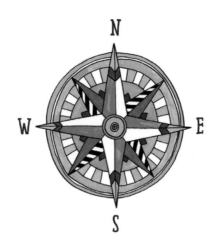

First published in the UK in 2019 by

Ivy Kids

An imprint of The Quarto Group
The Old Brewery
6 Blundell Street
London N7 9BH
United Kingdom
www.QuartoKnows.com

British Library Cataloguing-in-Publication Data
A catalogue record for this book is available from the British Library.

ISBN: 978-1-78240-787-4

This book was conceived, designed & produced by

Ivy Kids

58 West Street, Brighton BN1 2RA, United Kingdom

PUBLISHER	David Breuer
MANAGING EDITOR	Susie Behar
ART DIRECTOR	Hanri van Wyk
DESIGNER	Tilly
IN-HOUSE DESIGNER	Kate Haynes
EDITORS	Hazel Songhurst, Lucy Menzies & Hannah Dove

Manufactured in Guangdong, China TT072019

1 3 5 7 9 10 8 6 4 2

Tilly is an illustrator based in Brighton, UK. With an eye for
detail and a passion for map-making, she has drawn many of the
world's cities. Her favourites include Beijing, London and Paris.
Find more of her work at www.runningforcrayons.co.uk.